FURNESS RAILWAY LOCOMOTIVE No. 20

The Story So Far

Tim Ow

Contents

1. Introduction 2
2. In the beginning 3
3. The Furness Railway is Born 4
4. The Sharp, Stewart Tender Locomotives 5
5. Barrow's Iron and Steelworks 9
6. Retirement 12
7. Restoration 14
8. The Preservation Era 24
9. Gallery 37
10. Behind the Scenes 45
11. Timeline 46
12. What Next? 48

Furness Railway Trust CIO
Registered Charity No. 1163073

1. Introduction

The story of Furness Railway No 20's varied history, from its beginnings on the Furness Railway to its restoration to operational condition in January 1999, has already been told in the book *The Great Survivor*, published jointly in 1999 by the Cumbrian Railways Association and the Furness Railway Trust. This is long out of print having sold some 3,000 copies. However, Furness Railway No. 20 has been operational at heritage railways throughout Britain over the past 26 years, appeared on television and the big screen and also made thousands of friends. The locomotive's career has been nothing short of remarkable, having had a working career of 97 years with both the Furness Railway and Barrow's Iron and Steelworks before being a local landmark, spending 23 years in a school playground. It has then gone on to operate at many heritage railways and play a starring role at steam galas throughout Britain; it has also been the resident operational locomotive at the National Railway Museum's outpost at Locomotion, Shildon for nine years.

For those closely involved with the locomotive over the past 26 years it has been nothing short of life changing, with countless friends being made and many pleasurable experiences which will be remembered forever.

In this year 2025, the 200th anniversary of the opening of the first public railway between Stockton and Darlington on the 27th September 1825, it is felt time to bring FR 20's story up to date.

The purpose of this publication therefore is to summarise the locomotive's early history and restoration and then to recount its more recent activities and adventures. It is also an opportunity to showcase some of the wonderful photographs that have been taken during the locomotive's travels.

Tim Owen
Cark-in-Cartmel
Cumbria
May 2025

2. In the Beginning

Present day Barrow-in-Furness, with a population of 65,000, has an international reputation for the manufacture of high-tech nuclear powered submarines. However, in the early 1840s it was but a small fishing hamlet with a population of around 200 people. The catalyst for the transformation of the area however was not the creation of a shipyard, but the rich deposits of haematite ore in the Furness area which led to a demand for both labour and transport.

A number of local furnaces had been established in the 18th century including those at Newland and Backbarrow, but some of the excavated ore was also moved by horse and cart to various loading points along the north of Morecambe Bay where the cargo could be transferred to boats and shipped to South Wales for smelting. However, as mining developed it became clear that local roads, from the mines to the piers, were inadequate for the increasing amounts of ore mined and so a bill was passed in May 1844 for the construction of the Furness Railway. Meanwhile, the prospector, HW Schneider, had been in pursuance of a far larger quantity of ore which he eventually found at Park in 1850; this had a dramatic effect on the scale of the mining industry in the area.

The town of Barrow-in-Furness has since gone from strength to strength, becoming a major centre of iron and steel production until the 1980s as well as the major shipbuilding facility that it is today. However, it was the coming of the railways that finally enabled Barrow and the surrounding Furness area to flourish, providing an invaluable conduit that transformed the local economy and also brought with it the young locomotive engineer, James Ramsden (later Sir James Ramsden), who was to play a vital part in Barrow's development and become the first Mayor of Barrow-in-Furness.

3. The Furness Railway is Born

The initial 14 miles of the Railway was isolated from the rest of the rail network, its task essentially being to move the iron ore and Furness slate to the coast. Although initially envisaged being worked by horse power, the Board ordered two four-coupled bar framed tender steam locomotives from Bury, Curtis and Kennedy in 1845, which assisted construction works, and these were soon joined by a further two locomotives, Nos. 3 and 4, in 1846. No. 3, known as *Coppernob*, survives to this day in the care of the National Railway Museum, having had a working career of 52 years before being exhibited outside Barrow station until May 1941 when it suffered damage during the 'Barrow Blitz'.

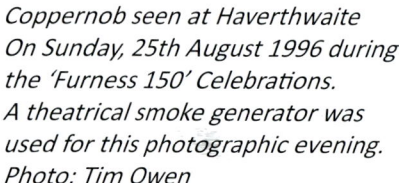

Coppernob seen at Haverthwaite On Sunday, 25th August 1996 during the 'Furness 150' Celebrations. A theatrical smoke generator was used for this photographic evening.
Photo: Tim Owen

The Railway opened for its first freight train, from Dalton to Barrow, on the 3rd June 1846 before formal clearance was given by the Board of Trade inspector for the operation of passenger services, which commenced on the 24th August that year. These first four locomotives then supplied all the motive power needs of the Furness Railway for the next six years.

However, as the iron ore trade blossomed, so did the Railway and the line was gradually extended to the north and then, via the Ulverstone and Lancaster Railway in 1857, to the south. The locomotive fleet was similarly expanded, with 2-2-2 well tanks being purchased from Sharp Brothers of Manchester for the operation of passenger services and more 0-4-0 tender locomotives from Fairbairn of Manchester, which had taken over their manufacture from Bury, Curtis & Kennedy when the firm closed in 1850.

4. The Sharp, Stewart 0-4-0 Tender Locomotives

Output from the mines continued to rise rapidly, from 100,000 tons in the mid-1840s to 700,000 tons in 1864. With a fleet still of only 16 locomotives by 1861, a significantly enlarged railway to operate and increased ore traffic, the Furness Railway sought a further four tender locomotives.

Whilst the Stockton & Darlington Railway had been using six-wheeled locomotives as long ago as the mid-1840s, the Furness Railway had continued to remain loyal to the 0-4-0 configuration that was to serve it well for over 50 years. The 0-4-0s were eminently suitable for accessing the many sidings which served the mines, the lifeblood of the Railway. Richard Mason, who took over from James Ramsden as locomotive engineer, was known to hold them in high regard and woe betide anyone who questioned their ability.

So, on the 23rd December 1862, the company placed an order with Sharp, Stewart & Co of Manchester for the provision of four 0-4-0 tender locomotives at a cost of £2,410.31 each. These were to be of Sharp, Stewart's own design with wrought iron plate frames and with a rectangular round-topped firebox, a change from the 'haystack' firebox design and bar frames that had typified the appearance of the earlier tender locomotives. Boiler pressure was to be 120 psi which, with a cylinder diameter of 15.5" and surprisingly large driving wheels of 4' 9", gave a tractive effort of 10,317 lbs. The boiler was to be the standard Sharp, Stewart diameter of 3' 10" and 11' 2" long, with 141 brass tubes of 2" diameter. This was to give a heating area of 898.75 square feet.

The order, No. 440 shown overleaf, states that the engine's tyres, axles, piston rods and crank pins, together with the tender tyres, were to be of Krupp's steel. The drawings for the engine (SS 1028) and tender (1218), were signed off by a Mr. Bottomley.

The tenders had a capacity of 1,200 gallons and two tons of coal and were of the same basic design that was to be delivered with the many larger locomotives from Sharp, Stewart in later years. The tenders delivered to the Furness Railway are distinguished by the slightly lower footplate area, which curves down from the coal space behind. They were notable for the box at the back of the water tank which probably contained re-railing jacks. The only brakes on the locomotive were located on the tender and operated by hand. It is believed that Sharp, Stewart delivered the locomotives without tender weather boards and that these were fitted by the Furness Railway on those locomotives that worked lines without a turntable. Although it was initially expected that the first two locomotives would be delivered in May 1863, it was in fact the 1st and 6th August before SS Nos. 1434 and 1435 (FR Nos. 17 and 18) arrived followed by No. 1447 (FR No. 19) on the 10th August and 1448 (FR No. 20) on the 21st August 1863.

Two subsequent orders for these 0-4-0 tender locomotives were made with deliveries of Nos. 25 and 26 in 1865 and then Nos. 27 and 28 in 1866. A further order of four locomotives (FR Nos. 29 to 32) was subsequently cancelled and replaced by four Sharp, Stewart 0-6-0 tender locomotives, the first of an eventual class of 55 such locomotives.

Nos. 27 and 28 were finally withdrawn from service in 1918 after a working life of 52 years. However, fate determined that the first six locomotives were soon to have a more eventful change of career.

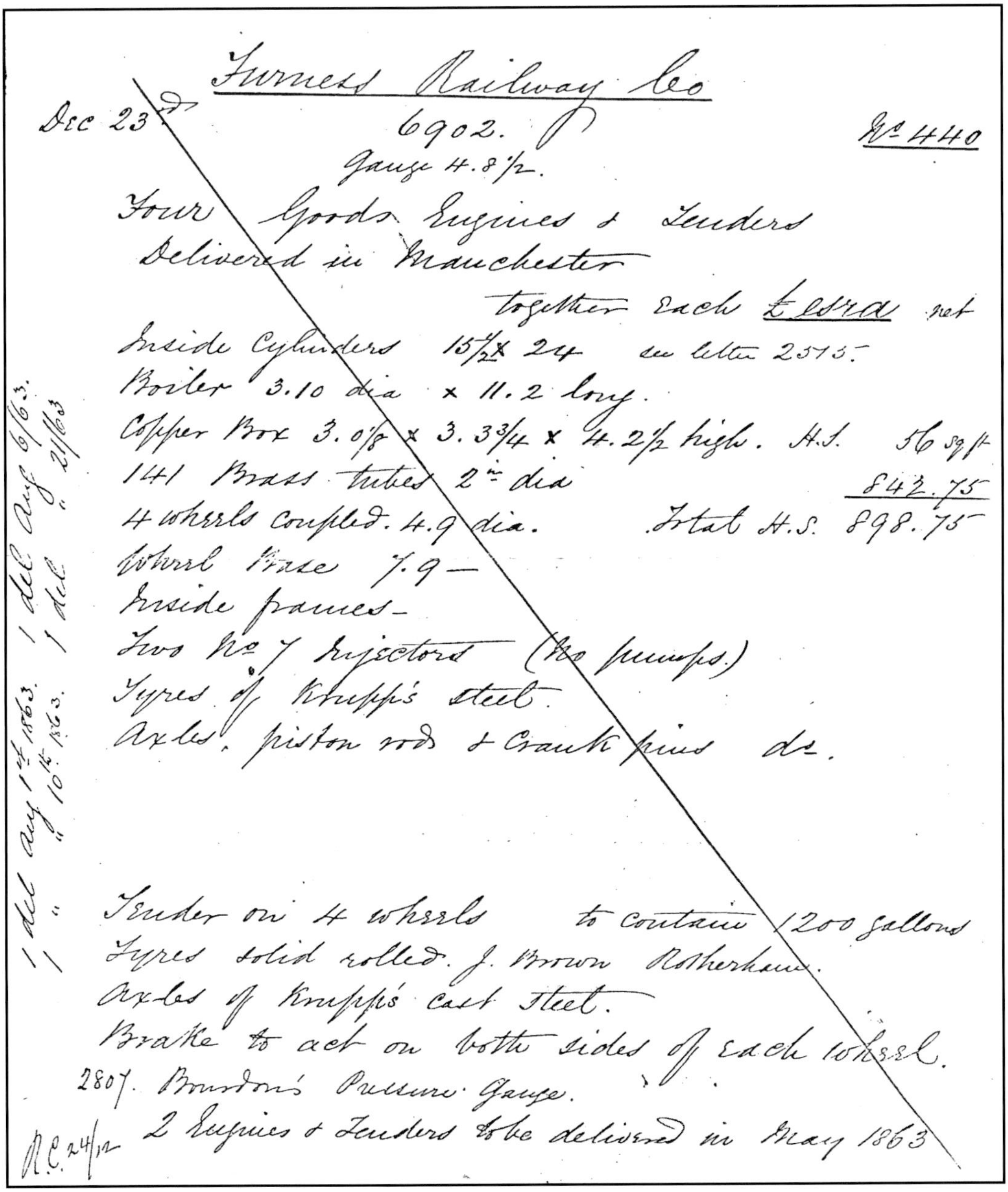

Dec 23rd

<u>Furness Railway Co</u>
6902.
Gauge 4.8½.

№ 440

Four Goods Engines & Tenders
Delivered in Manchester
together each £ 2574 net
Inside Cylinders 15½ x 24   in letter 2515.
Boiler 3.10 dia x 11.2 long.
Copper Box 3.0⅛ x 3.3¾ x 4.2½ high. H.S. 56 sq ft
141 Brass tubes 2" dia   842.75
4 wheels coupled. 4.9 dia.   Total H.S. 898.75
Wheel Base 7.9 —
Inside frames —
Two No 7 Injectors (No pumps.)
Tyres of Krupp's steel.
Axles, piston rods & Crank pins do.

Tender on 4 wheels   to contain 1200 gallons
Tyres solid rolled. J. Brown Rotherham.
Axles of Krupp's cast steel.
Brake to act on both sides of each wheel.
2807. Bourdon's Pressure Gauge.

R.C. 24/12   2 Engines & Tenders to be delivered in May 1863

1 del Aug 1st 1863. 1 del Aug 6/63.
1 del " 10th 1863.   "   2/63

The page is from the Sharp, Stewart order book giving details of Order No. 440 for four 0-4-0 tender goods engines. Set out on the page is a rather detailed description of the engines and this page, with the drawings, would be the starting point of the construction of the engines destined for the Furness Railway. The line struck across the page presumably denotes the fact that the order had been fulfilled.

Courtesy: Mitchell Library

This fine study of FR locomotive No.27 taken in Barrow Yard depicts how FR 20 would have looked before conversion to a saddle tank locomotive. It formed a prime reference for the development of plans for the reconstruction of BHSCo. No. 7.
Photo: LPC Collection Ref. 14639, courtesy National Railway Museum

Before and After

One of the Furness Railway Sharp Stewart 0-4-0 locomotives after conversion to a saddle tank configuration and transfer to the Barrow Haematite Steel Co., seen posed with staff at Park Mines in about 1880.
Photo: Barrow Archive Centre Ref. BDP37

5. Barrow's Iron and Steelworks

Given the scale of mining in the area it then made sense for Barrow to have its own ironworks, the first blast furnaces opening in 1859, followed by the creation of the Barrow Haematite Steel Co Ltd in 1864 which started producing steel ingots in 1865. The development of the Bessemer plant there made Barrow one of the largest steel producers in the world.

A view of Barrow's Iron and Steelworks taken from Walney Road.
Photo: Barrow Archive Centre Ref. LC200 PA/IRO20

Such a large undertaking, however, itself required steam locomotives of its own to move the ore and products around the large site at Hindpool. With the Furness Railway needing more powerful 0-6-0 locomotives to handle its growing freight traffic, a deal was done whereby the BHSCo purchased the first six relatively new Sharp, Stewart 0-4-0 engines (Nos. 17-20 and 25/26), from the Furness Railway without their tenders at a price of £1,550 each. The Directors of the FR agreed the sale on the 25th May 1870, but it is thought that Nos. 25 and 26 were not actually transferred to the BHSCo until 1873. It is understood that all the engines were converted to saddle tank engines by Sharp, Stewart, and that the tenders were allocated to the new replacement 0-6-0 locomotives. The addition of saddle tanks for water required that the Salter safety valves be turned at an angle of 90 degrees with the springs being attached to the side of the new water tank that had been placed on the boiler.

There is continuing mystery as to the allocation of BHSCo locomotive fleet numbers to the engines transferred from the Furness Railway. It had always been assumed that the numbers were allocated as follows

SS No.	FR No.	BHSCo No.
1434	17	5
1435	18	7
1447	19	8
1448	20	16
1585	25	17
1586	26	18

Subsequent events proved that the above assumptions were incorrect with No. 7 later found during restoration to be the former FR No. 20.

Most of these little saddle-tank engines were re-built at some stage during their careers with BHSCo, being given smaller 4' 0" driving wheels, which increased their tractive effort – apart from No. 7 which retained its 4' 9" wheels. New 120 psi boilers were fitted with Ramsbottom safety valves, with No. 7 being rebuilt in 1915, again at the age of 52 years.

The appearance of the engine was significantly changed with the addition of a cab, plus the new boiler had a dome positioned mid-way along the boiler. No. 7's larger driving wheels, which gave more speed, made it the favoured locomotive to move the hot metal wagons from the blast furnaces to the Mixer, a large gas-heated storage reservoir for molten pig iron situated at the north end of the ironworks. At some point the diameter of the cylinders was increased to 16" giving a new theoretical tractive effort of 10, 995 lbs, a six per cent increase.

A view of No. 7 after its 1915 rebuild. The bent spokes referred to in the text can clearly be seen. Photo: Sankey Collection Photo CB12 BDP 86/1/7051

Nationalisation of the steelworks in 1942 and its transfer to the Ministry of Supply saw the locomotive fleet being split, with No. 7 being allocated to the steelworks by the still privately owned BHSCo on the basis of an unfavourable boiler report for No. 7 which identified that *landings of the copper firebox are fractured and leaking very badly.*

Despite its firebox problems, No. 7 continued in service at the steelworks until diesels took over the work on the 9th July 1960. In the meantime, the locomotive had received new wheelsets, the spokes of which had become bent through sheer hard work, and adjustments to its injectors.

6. Retirement

No. 7 being loaded up at Barrow Steelworks for delivery to the George Hastwell Special School, Abbey Road, Barrow-in-Furness.
Photo: Ken Royall

Nos. 7 and 17 were the last steam locomotives in service at the steelworks and it must be concluded that these former Furness Railway engines had gained some degree of affection for they were both given new homes, No. 7 to the George Hastwell School in Abbey Road, Barrow, whilst No. 17 was taken to the Stonecross Special School in Ulverston. Fortunately, the steelworks expended some effort to ensure that both locomotives were complete and spruced up before being taken to their new homes. No. 7 was probably the more well known, with its position in the playground close to the main Abbey Road in Barrow, and a generation of schoolchildren played on it. No. 17 was in a more secluded position in Ulverston.

However, after 23 years exposed to the elements, No. 7 was purchased by Ian Atkinson, then General Manager at Steamtown, Carnforth, and Lance Wooff, who moved it to Steamtown in November 1983. It was then joined by No. 17 after Ian and Lance were given custodianship of the engine.

A delightful photograph of children with No. 7 in the grounds of the George Hastwell School, Abbey Road, Barrow-in-Furness.
Photo: Ken Royall

Work immediately commenced on stripping down No. 7 with the intention of returning it to its 1863 configuration, but the scheme came to a halt with the untimely death of Lance and Ian's resignation from Steamtown. The Lakeside Railway Society, which had been the voluntary workforce which had assisted the reopening of the Lakeside & Haverthwaite Railway in 1973, had always kept an eye on both the former Furness Railway engines and stepped in to buy the components of No. 7 in 1990 for the sum of £5,000, with little publicity given the unfortunate events that had led to the sale. With the Society already heavily committed to the restoration of former Great Western Railway 0-6-2T No. 5643, there were some who questioned the wisdom of this latest purchase. However, on the 25th October, a new body, the Furness Railway Trust, which had been set up to further such restoration projects and which could attract both grants and tax concession, was granted charitable status, which was a key step to achieving the eventual restoration of No. 7.

7. Restoration

Early Efforts

With the Furness Railway Trust's finances already committed to the restoration of GWR No. 5643, there was little initial progress with No. 7. The first task was to commission a professional examination of the boiler and firebox, which found that these had reached the end of their working lives. The components of the engine had been scattered around the site at Steamtown so a thorough search took place and an inventory was created. There was some good news with the discovery that the general arrangement drawings for Sharp, Stewart order no. 440 were held at the Science Museum, which were later to prove invaluable and enabled an outline specification for a new boiler to be produced by Trustee Norman Gard. It was accepted that the locomotive's second boiler had been deemed to be beyond economic repair and was in any case of the wrong outline for an 1863 re-build project.

The new fabrication made at Longridge to enable No. 7 to be converted to a tender locomotive. Photo: Alan Middleton

The Trust did receive some funding from Norman for some initial work on the chassis to facilitate the conversion back to a tender locomotive. This took place at Longridge, however, when this work had been completed the frames were placed back into storage, temporarily at Lytham.

Raising Funds

The scheme was re-awoken through proposals to celebrate the 150th anniversary of the Furness Railway in 1996, and in 1995 well known Ravenglass & Eskdale driver Peter van Zeller approached the FRT to offer assistance in obtaining grant funding. Trust Chairman Tim Owen along with fellow Trustees Alan Middleton and Fergus MacGregor prepared detailed costings which enabled the PRISM Fund of the Science Museum to award a grant of £10,768 to the conservation of the original chassis. A successful application was then made to the relatively new Heritage Lottery Fund which yielded a grant of £97,500, which was publicly announced at a ceremony at Barrow Station on Saturday, 24th August 1996 which commemorated the 150th anniversary of the Furness Railway's first passenger train.

The Barrow Shipyard

The FRT had set itself an ambitious timescale of two years to restore BHSCo No. 7 back to its original Furness Railway condition, which would require a new boiler, tender and many other fittings. It was now important to find a suitable workshop with the necessary facilities to undertake the work. An approach was made to Vickers Shipbuilding & Engineering Ltd (VSEL) to undertake the work with guidance and project management being undertaken by FRT personnel. The Shipyard had previously undertaken work on both steam and diesel locomotives in its past, including the overhaul of LNER 'Pacific' Flying Scotsman in 1978. With the HLF contract finally signed on the 8th October, and after some successful persuasion with the shipyard, the chassis and most other existing components of No.7 were moved to Barrow for the restoration to commence.

The first task undertaken was to sand blast the frames and it was then that the original maker's numbers were spotted, confirming that the locomotive that had previously been thought of as Furness Railway No. 18 was in fact Furness Railway No. 20. The frames were then painted in red oxide primer and transferred to the appropriately named Engine Shop.

March 1997 saw the driving wheels finally liberated from store at Steamtown, Carnforth, and then subsequently transferred to Hunslet-Barclay at Kilmarnock for tyre turning.

One of the potential show stoppers in the restoration was the poor condition of the valve faces and for which there was no suitable mechanical planer in the shipyard nor in the locality. Fortunately, a machine, with the required reach of 22", was found at the Severn Valley Railway and their personnel came to Barrow with the machine to undertake this vital work.

A New Boiler and Tender

Meanwhile, the FRT had arranged a contract with Israel Newton & Sons of Idle, Bradford for the construction of a new boiler and firebox, considered then to be the biggest new boiler in railway preservation.

The new boiler for FR 20 takes shape in the works of Israel Newton & Sons, Idle, Bradford. Photo: Tim Owen

Thoughts were then turned to the construction of a new tender. Whilst the outline general arrangement drawings were of great help, there were no detailed drawings and therefore a considerable amount of time had to be spent producing drawings for individual components such as the tender chassis, tank, spring hangers, axleboxes and draw gear, to name but a few. This work, using Computer Aided Design (CAD), was undertaken at the home of Fergus MacGregor in Kendal during evenings and weekends. Many miles were then covered in sending the drawings to pattern makers, visiting foundries and then taking castings to machine shops.

The Shipyard agreed to manufacture the tender chassis using the drawings provided on a disc – a far cry from the methods of 1863! It was then necessary to find someone to manufacture the tender superstructure which would accommodate 1,200 gallons of water and two tons of coal. An appointment was made with Maggie Chadwick, Principal of Furness College, to enquire whether the College would undertake this part of the project as a training exercise at its Channelside base in Barrow. This was then agreed on the basis that the FRT would provide the components and pay for a project manager, Alan Greenwood, who was a retired member of staff. This proved to be an excellent arrangement for both parties.

The FRT was fortunate to have obtained two wheelsets for the tender which had come up for sale. These originated from the former Buxton snowploughs (known in the railway fraternity as *Snow King* and *Snow Queen*) which had been purchased for another locomotive building project and were of LNER manufacture. It had been decided that a vacuum brake should be fitted to the tender to meet modern regulations and the FRT was fortunate in receiving an offer from member George Fletcher to undertake the necessary design work.

Another issue that had to be addressed was the manufacture of the distinctive large bell mouthed dome cover for the boiler. Specialist metal spinners came in with a £2,000 quote just for the tooling costs and so FRT engineer Alan Middleton offered to undertake the work at a much reduced cost, using over 50 pieces of metal skilfully fashioned into shape.

Finishing the Project

There was a difficult moment in the project when VSEL, on the 12th December 1997, announced that it was pulling out of commercial heavy engineering work at the end of March 1998. However, with many of the locomotive's components already in the Shipyard, it was agreed that a sensible solution would be for the FRT to provide its own resources to complete the project using the facilities in the Engine Shop. From the 7th April 1998 Alan Middleton and Tim Owen took on the main work at Barrow assisted by other FRT members as and when they were able to lend time to the project. In particular, mention must be made of the physical assistance rendered by Brian Murray, Ian Camfield. John Dixon, George Fletcher, David Rimmer and Phil Cousins. VSEL managers Neil Johnson, Tom Jefferson, Kevin Brockbank and Jon Wilkinson (himself a steam driver and FRT member) made the necessary arrangements to ensure that the project ran as smoothly as possible. The staff in the Engine Shop were always welcoming and helpful and the project received great assistance from driller Vince Smith who spent many of his lunchtimes using specialist air tools to drill the numerous holes required, particularly on the new tender chassis, which had arrived from the New Assembly Shop on the 21st May.

There had been good progress at Furness College with the new tender tank and it was handed over to the FRT on the 15th May. The Trust had been fortunate in that Fergus MacGreor had spotted a photograph in the Continental Railway Journal of an 1888 Sharp, Stewart tender that resided at the Efis Museum, Çamlik in Turkey. Vital design detail was then obtained through the good offices of Alan Prior, a Briton who conveniently lived near Çamlik and who had taken the photograph.

Another key milestone for the project took place at Idle on the 15th June when the new boiler successfully passed its hydraulic test at 240 psi. It had been built to modern standards, which assumed a maximum working pressure of 160 psi, although it was not the intention of the FRT to work it above 120 psi.

The delays caused by change in responsibility for completing the project led to National Heritage Memorial Fund project monitor Richard Gibbon, of the National Railway Museum, recommending that an additional six months should be allowed for the project to be completed i.e. end of January 1999. This concentrated the minds of everyone and long hours were worked to achieve the deadline.

The new tender tank being collected from Furness College.
Photo: Tim Owen

VSEL cut and assembled the chassis frame for the new tender. The chassis is shown after arrival in the Engine Shop.
Photo: Furness Railway Trust

The new boiler was brought over from Idle to Haverthwaite where it was united with its new chimney and steam tested to 140 psi on the 31st July 1998, witnessed by Gordon Newton (Israel Newton & Sons), Sam Foster (Halcrow Transmark) and Jerry Bayley (Royal Sun & Alliance Engineering), before being transported onwards to the Shipyard.

The author takes final measurements before the boiler is lowered onto the frames. Photo: Marconi Marine

After much effort, the main components of the engine began to materialise with the new tender chassis fitted onto its wheels on the 26th August and the boiler being fitted onto the engine frames on the 8th September. The next three months saw a great deal of activity to turn these main components into a working steam locomotive with a decision being made to move FR 20 out of the workshop to Haverthwaite before the Christmas close down of the Shipyard.

A transporter was ordered for the 17th December and FR 20 was greeted on departure at Traffic Gate by an interested crowd and local press to see the

The finishing touches to the paintwork are applied by Tim Owen and Phil Cousins.
Photo: Geoff Holme

The day of departure. Left to right: VSEL driller Vince Smith, Alan Middleton and Tim Owen with the completed locomotive in the Engine Shop on Thursday, 17th December 1998.
Photo: Marconi Marine

locomotive emerge into public view for the first time. There was similar interest at Haverthwaite when the tender and then the engine arrived separately during the day, to be coupled up and shunted into the main shed there.

Work continued over the Christmas period and, on the 8th January, FR 20 was drawn out of the shed for a fire to be lit. There was huge relief and joy when the regulator was finally opened and the locomotive moved under its own steam for the first time.

Commissioning

A successful formal steam test took place at Haverthwaite on the 13th January 1999 in sleet and snow under the unexpected gaze of television cameras, and this was followed by an impromptu return trip to Lakeside with a brake van. The TV footage, confirming a successful steaming, allowed the FRT to complete its documentation with the Heritage Lottery Fund and, with relief, claim the final drawdown of the grant.

Trial running of FR 20 on the bank at Backbarrow on the Lakeside & Haverthwaite Railway on the 9th February 1999.
Photo: Tim Owen

Further light engine test runs took place in February followed by a run with two Mark 1 coaches to commission the vacuum brake system.

Alan Middleton holds the umbrella for Lady Grania Cavendish during the ceremony at Haverthwaite to mark the introduction into service of the restored locomotive on the 20th April 1999. Tim Owen (left) and John Dixon look on.
Photo: Ken Royall

A formal launch, in dreadful weather, was held at Haverthwaite on Tuesday, 20th April attended by Lady Grania Cavendish, whose husband's family had been prominent promoters of the Furness Railway in in the 1840s. The return journey to Lakeside, watched by flag waving children at the nearby Backbarrow School, included a memorable run past at Newby Bridge, and was enjoyed by the many guests who included representatives of businesses that had manufactured and repaired components for the locomotive.

What Next?

The original book which recorded the history and restoration of FR 20, *The Great Survivor*, published in 1999 by the Furness Railway Trust and the Cumbrian Railways Association, concluded that it was surely unlikely that FR 20's future career could be anything like as remarkable as the first 136 years of its life. The next sections of this book will surely question the veracity of this statement!

8. The Preservation Era

Victorian Evenings

Now that the locomotive had proved itself, thoughts were turned as to how best to use it and show it off to the public. It was too small to operate the Lakeside & Haverthwaite Railway's daily summer passenger service and the FRT had been advised by Richard Gibbon during restoration that it would be inappropriate for FR 20 to be used as a service train loco. However, it was thought there would be a market for a weekly evening Victorian themed trip to Lakeside during the main school holidays. And so began ten years of memorable Victorian evenings, which included run pasts at Newby Bridge and which were then extended to include a trip on the Furness Railway built lake steamer *MV Tern*, constructed in 1891.

The consist of the train was enhanced in 2003 with the completion of the restoration of the FRT's North London Railway four-wheeled carriage which added to the Victorian travel experience. Victorian dress was encouraged and the evenings were regularly attended by Queen Victoria herself along with companion, John Brown! Those enjoying a pre-journey meal at Haverthwaite were usually serenaded by 78 rpm vinyl records on wind up Gramophones.

2000 Off to Yorkshire

The year 2000 brought a request for FR 20 to visit the Keighley & Worth Valley Railway in May, including operating shuttle trains between Keighley and Ingrow, and its first photo charter. There had been strong links between the L&HR and the K&WVR in the early years when Lakeside Railway Society volunteers had been given the opportunity to train as drivers and firemen prior to the opening of the L&HR in 1973. It was, therefore, appropriate that FR 20 should make its first trip away to Haworth.

Later in the summer the producers of a forthcoming big screen movie, *Possession* starring Gwyneth Paltrow, made contact to secure the use of FR 20 in September for filming on the North Yorkshire Moors Railway. Set in 1859 on the Whitby & Pickering Railway, FR 20 was the closest operational locomotive which could replicate the required railway scenes and it was paired up with four 6-wheeled carriages.

Train crew and passengers pose with FR 20 at Newby Bridge Station with the Victorian Evening train on the 26th August 2003.

Passengers gather to board the Victorian Evening train at Haverthwaite on the 9th August 2005.
Photos: both Alan Johnstone

One day of filming took place at Pickering whilst some moving shots were filmed at Moorgates bridge where the train and a modern car had to cross at the same time.

Once the filming had been completed, there came a request from the NYMR for the loco to stay on to take part in the three-day Autumn Steam Gala where, with two of the 6-wheeled coaches, it operated three return trips a day between Pickering and Levisham.

2001 East Midlands Tour

April 2001 saw FR 20 set off to Barrow Hill Roundhouse Railway Centre to take part in a two-day open weekend. There it top and tailed two brake vans, sometimes with Freightliner diesel No. 57 011, giving rides to visitors. There was a break at lunchtime to allow the loco to take centre stage on the turntable in the magnificent roundhouse. Highlight of the weekend was the opportunity to give a footplate ride to the Duke of Devonshire, a direct descendant of one of the main promoters of the Furness Railway.

FR 20 then moved to the Midland Railway Centre at Butterley where it operated with a set of the railway's marvellous Victorian carriages and it also undertook another photo charter.

2004 Railfest

The first Railfest at the National Railway Museum in York took place during the late May Bank Holiday week and was deemed to be a great success. FR 20 was in steam all nine days, with its crew welcoming hundreds of visitors onto its footplate. It was then requested to haul the two-coach passenger shuttle for the Thursday and Friday. It was an emotional occasion for the FR 20 team to see what had been a playground ornament having the opportunity to operate in front of the crowds at the NRM.

2007-2008 First Ten Year Overhaul

After nine years in service, mainly at the Lakeside & Haverthwaite Railway, the FRT decided to utilise the winter period of 2007/2008 to undertake the first ten-year boiler overhaul of the locomotive. As the locomotive had only run for nine relatively undemanding years since its re-build, it was decided that little other than the boiler overhaul itself was required. This necessitated the removal of the boiler, extrication of the 148 tubes and a non-destructive test of the boiler and firebox. All was found to be well and the locomotive was test steamed on the 24th July 2008, in time for what turned out to be the last Victorian Evenings at Haverthwaite in August.

2008 North East Tour

The Trust received a proposition to take part in a three-weekend tour of the north east in September 2008, along with veteran 0-6-0WT locomotive *Bellerophon*, which was built at the Haydock Foundry in 1874. The first weekend would be spent at the Tanfield Railway, followed by a visit to the National Railway Museum's outpost, *Locomotion* at Shildon, and then finally three steaming at Beamish Open Air Museum, including a photographic charter. This proved highly successful and heavily influenced the next ten years of FR 20's life.

2009 – 2018 *Locomotion*, Shildon

On the 22nd February 2009 FR 20 was transported to *Locomotion* with the offer of around 30 steamings throughout the year. The Museum had a 0.4 mile long demonstration line and provided footplate experience days as well as passenger rides in brake vans on the demonstration line. This proved to be ideal work for what was a 'museum engine that worked'. The October half term holiday saw FR 20 move to the NRM at York to provide nine days of passenger running on the demonstration line. The arrangement for FR 20's stay of over nine years residency at *Locomotion* worked well for both parties, with campervan accommodation on site allowed for FRT representatives. Many friends and contacts were made and FR 20 worked alongside many famous locomotives there during its stay. This included the six surviving Gresley A4 'Pacifics' which assembled at Shildon in February 2014 for the 'Great Goodbye'. FR 20 'top and tailed' brake van rides with Gresley A3 'Pacific' No. 4472 *Flying Scotsman* and also came face to face with new build A1 'Pacific' No. 60163 *Tornado*.

The loyal FRT maintenance team, with assistance from *Locomotion* staff and volunteers, undertook the necessary maintenance work which successfully saw FR 20 through its annual boiler examinations, albeit 100 miles away from its home base of Preston.

The arrangement with *Locomotion* was flexible, which allowed the engine to make visits to other heritage railway sites.

FR 20 had many varied and famous shed mates whilst at Locomotion, Shildon. Here it is seen with the National Railway Museum replica of Rocket (the original built in 1829) and also new build A1 'Pacific' 4-6-2 No. 60163 Tornado, completed in 2008.

Photos: both Tim Owen

2010 – 2011 'Golden Oldies' and Other Visits

The Great Central Railway staged the first of two 'Golden Oldie' Galas in 2010, which was attended by the *Planet* and *Rocket* replicas as well as Beattie 2-4-0WT No. 30585 and Manning Wardle 0-6-0ST *Sir Berkeley* of 1890. FR 20 was then off to Beamish again for nearly two months of regular weekend steamings. Here it paired up with the FRT's Great Eastern Railway royal saloon No. 5 of 1898 to make a real vintage ride for visitors. The loco then set off for its furthest venture south, to the Bluebell Railway in Sussex where it was the only visiting locomotive to take part in the Bluebell's 50th Anniversary celebrations. Its prime duty was to propel the L&NWR Directors Observation Saloon of 1913 from Kingscote up to the Imberhorne tip, which was still to be excavated to allow the line to extend to East Grinstead. 2011 saw FR 20 return to the Great Central Railway at the end of May for a second 'Golden Oldies' Gala.

2012 – A Memorable Tour

Sometimes fate aligns opportunities which allow an exciting itinerary, and so FR 20 set off from *Locomotion* to appear at its new home depot, the Ribble Steam Railway, where it operated services at the February Steam Gala and throughout April. It then moved to the Midland Railway Centre for a short stay before heading off to Kidderminster for the 'Kidderminster 150' celebrations. Here there was an unscripted surprise when it was called upon to haul a Great Western Railway saloon from Kidderminster to Bewdley with no lesser personage than the Duke of Gloucester on board! FR 20 then set off to the NRM at York for the 2012 Railfest where it was in steam for nine days before heading off to the Bluebell Railway again where it was to haul that fateful train of 9th June 1865 which derailed at Staplehurst with Charles Dickens on board. This was, of course, a re-enactment for the big screen cameras, directed by Ralph Fiennes, and came to the cinemas under the title *The Invisible Woman*. Three days of filming were fitted in before the locomotive was whisked away to the Middleton Railway at Leeds for the Railway's 200th Anniversary. Finally, FR 20 then returned to *Locomotion* to continue to operate services there for the remainder of 2012.

FR 20 about to haul a train on the demonstration line at Locomotion, Shildon, on the occasion of its 150th birthday.
Photo: Alan Johnstone

A special piece of coal for FR 20 on its birthday!
Photo: Tim Owen

2013 - Happy 150th Birthday!

The 21st August 2013 saw FR 20 mark the 150th anniversary of its delivery to the Furness Railway. A special day of celebration was organised and *Locomotion* did the locomotive proud with free rides given to visitors, a garland of flowers for the engine and a birthday cake. There was also a special piece of coal for FR 20 itself! Later in the year the locomotive went to the Tyseley Open Weekend in October before returning to *Locomotion*.

2015 Off to Bonnie Scotland

FR 20's furthest venture north so far has been to the Bo'ness & Kinneil Railway where it made a splendid sight operating for two days between Bo'ness and Birkhill with two former Caledonian Railway coaches.

2018 – Goodbye to *Locomotion*

After over nine years based at *Locomotion*, Shildon, and with its ten-year boiler ticket due to end in July, it was agreed that FR 20's final steamings there would be over the early May Bank Holiday. Monday, 7th May, proved to be an emotional occasion with a lovely speech given by Anthony Coulls

Some cake cutting at Locomotion, Shildon, before FR 20 runs its last trains there on Monday, 7th May 2018.
Photo: Courtesy Locomotion, Shildon

on behalf of the National Railway Museum. Many volunteers who had worked with the FRT there over the years came back for one last ride behind the locomotive. And, yes, there was more cake! Thanks go to Dr. George Muirhead, Pam Porter, Richard Pearson and the staff and volunteers at *Locomotion* for making FR 20's stay there so special.

Two more final steamings took place at Preston over the weekend of the 7th and 8th July before the locomotive was withdrawn from operations for overhaul.

2018-2021 Second Ten Year Overhaul

FR 20's boiler is lifted clear of the frames in the Ribble Steam Railway's workshop on the 27th October 2018 in preparation for a non-destructive test and re-tubing.
Photo: Tim Owen

The first ten-year overhaul had been light in nature, but the more extensive use of FR 20 over the last ten years had yielded some niggles that the FRT team decided to tackle. To be fair, the 150 plus years old locomotive had performed very reliably over the past twenty years, but now was the time to put a few things right. Curiously these mainly involved the newer components that had been used during restoration.

Firstly, the two live steam valves that operated the two injectors had proved to be rather fragile in the hands of firemen used to bigger and more robust engines, with the spindle threads being stripped on a number of occasions. It was decided therefore to replace the valves with larger versions, which also allowed a greater flow of steam to the injectors and which subsequently proved to make them easier to operate.

FR 20's tender is lifted back onto its wheels at Preston on the 4th September 2019 after work on the bearings and journals.
Photo: Tim Owen

The other significant issue was the propensity for two of the brass tender axlebox bearings to run hot without warning and for no obvious reason. Numerous adjustments and examinations had proved fruitless and so it was decided to convert the bearings to have a white metal surface. The tender wheelsets were sent away to have the journals skimmed so allowing a fresh start. So far the conversion has proved to be a success.

All was going well with the overhaul until the unanticipated global Covid-19 epidemic which unexpectedly brought work to a halt in March 2020. Work was allowed to resume under strict conditions later in the year and the hydraulic test of the boiler eventually took place on the 12th October followed by an out of frames steaming on the 16th November 2020.

2021 Return to Barrow-in-Furness and Return to Service

The splendid 5" gauge model of FR 20 constructed by Tom Jones of Seascale poses in front of the full sized version at the Dock Museum, Barrow on Saturday, 17th July 2021.
Photo: Tim Owen

The limitations on those allowed to work on FR 20 continued into 2021, but steady progress was achieved including the first complete re-paint of the engine since the original restoration. There was then great joy when FR 20 was invited to be a static exhibit at the Dock Museum, Barrow, for the Barrow Festival of Transport on the 17th July 2021. Although not quite yet in operable condition, the locomotive made a splendid sight on the back of a Reid Freight transporter which had been driven there by Simon Reid himself. The sun shone all day and many Barrovians came to share the occasion.

A formal steam test took place at Preston on the 11th October following which FR 20 returned to service for one day on the 23rd October.

2022 Back on the Road

This year was a relatively quiet reintroduction to traffic for FR 20 with it continuing to operate intermittently at the Ribble Steam Railway. However, there was a successful trip to the Buckinghamshire Railway Centre for the early May Bank Holiday weekend where it ran with three vintage carriages, which looked a treat with the old locomotive.

2023 Didcot and an Extended Holiday in South Wales

After running at the RSR's Spring Steam Gala, FR 20 headed south to the Didcot Railway Centre where it proved extremely popular during its nine days in steam. The loco then moved to Blaenavon's Heritage Railway, its first foray into Wales. The line is extremely steep and there was considerable disappointment when FR 20's right hand crosshead cotter sheared on the 1 in 24 grade approach to Furnace Sidings station on its first day in service. This caused damage to the right hand piston and front cylinder end cover. Fortunately, it proved possible to repair the locomotive through the good works of Ryan Pope and his team from the West Somerset Railway. The locomotive then stayed to complete a total of six steamings including an appearance at the Railway's excellent Autumn Steam Gala. The year marked the 160th birthday of the locomotive with yet another cake to celebrate.

2024 The South West and East Lancashire

The good relationship made with the West Somerset Railway in 2023 led to an invitation for FR 20 to take part in the celebrations to mark the 150th Anniversary of the opening on the 16th July 1874 of the Watchet to Minehead Railway. FR 20 was required to haul two Watchet to Minehead specials as well as operate shuttles in and out of Minehead station over a period of five days with Hawthorn Leslie 0-4-0ST *Marston Thompson and Evershed* of 1924.

The Autumn then saw FR 20 make the short trip from Preston to Bury to take part in the East Lancashire Railway's Autumn Steam Gala where it proved to be extremely popular, hauling trains between Bury and Ramsbottom.

2025

Another busy year has been scheduled for FR 20 starting with a very successful return visit to the Tanfield Railway where it starred in the Railway's first two weekends of the Great North Festival of Railways.

As well as working passenger services at the Ribble Steam Railway, the locomotive is scheduled to appear at 'The Greatest Gathering' at Derby at the beginning of August. A return to the East Lancashire Railway is planned for September and October.

The following chapter contains photographic memories of many of FR 20's visits to heritage railways throughout Britain.

9. Gallery

FR 20 and two Metropolitan Railway coaches exit Mytholmes Tunnel during a photo charter on the Keighley & Worth Valley Railway on the 15th May 2000.
Photo: Phil Cousins

FR 20 shunts its two-coach train at Levisham during the North Yorkshire Moors Railway's Autumn Steam Gala, October 2000.
Photo: Phil Cousins

FR 20 poses on the turntable in Barrow Hill Roundhouse, built 1870, on the 29th April 2001.
Photo: Tim Owen

FR 20 at the head of some loaned coaches from the Tanfield Railway poses alongside Marshall traction engine 'Lady Margaret' of 1889 during a photo charter at Beamish Museum on the 26th September 2008.
Photo: David Williams

FR 20 rubs shoulders with replica 2-2-0 Liverpool & Manchester Railway 'Planet' at the Great Central Railway's 'Golden Oldies' event on the 28th May 2010.
Photo: Tim Owen

FR 20 at Rowley Station, Beamish, on the 27th June 2010 with the FRT's Great Eastern Railway royal saloon No. 5 of 1898, which was built for Princess Alexandra.
Photo: Tim Owen

FR 20 with the Midland Railway Centre's rake of vintage coaches on the 6th May 2012.
Photo: Tim Owen

FR 20 at the site of Imberhorne tip whilst working shuttle trains from Kingscote with the L&NWR Directors Observation Saloon of 1913 during the Bluebell Railway's 50th Anniversary Gala on the 6th August 2010.
Photo: Tim Owen

FR 20 with two of the Bluebell Railway's beautiful wooden bodied coaches during a photo charter on the 12th August 2010.
Photo: Matt Allen

FR 20 heads two Caledonian Railway coaches on the Bo'ness & Kinneil Railway between Bo'ness and Birkhill on the 24th October 2015.
Photo: Ian Lothian

FR 20 stands in Quainton Road Station with its train of three vintage carriages on the 1st May 2022.
Photo: Tim Owen

FR 20 poses alongside GWR replica 2-2-2 Firefly, the original built in 1840, outside the Didcot Railway Centre transfer shed on the 16th April 2023.
Photo: Tim Owen

FR 20 approaches Furnace Sidings Station as it assists the final train of the Blaenavon Heritage Railway's Autumn Steam Gala on Sunday, 10th September 2023. Behind is Hawthorn Leslie 0-4-0ST Keighley Gas Works No. 2 and Andrew Barclay 0-4-0ST Caledonia Works.
Photo: Tim Owen

FR 20 hauls the 'Minehead 150' VIP Special near Kentsford on the West Somerset Railway on the 20th July 2024.
Photo: Mike Lanning

FR 20 crosses Brooksbottom Viaduct in beautiful autumnal sunshine on Friday, 11th October 2024 during the East Lancashire Railway's Autumn Steam Gala.
Photo: Harry Cain

FR 20 in action on the Tanfield Railway on the 3rd May 2025 during the Great North Festival of Railways.
Photo: Robert Batty

10. Behind the Scenes

Finally, we take a quick look at some of the work that goes on out of public sight to present FR 20 in pristine condition for service and also a taste of some of the less glamorous but essential work:

FR 20 is cleaned, polished and oiled up for service outside the historic Marley Hill engine shed on the Tanfield Railway.
Photo: Tim Owen

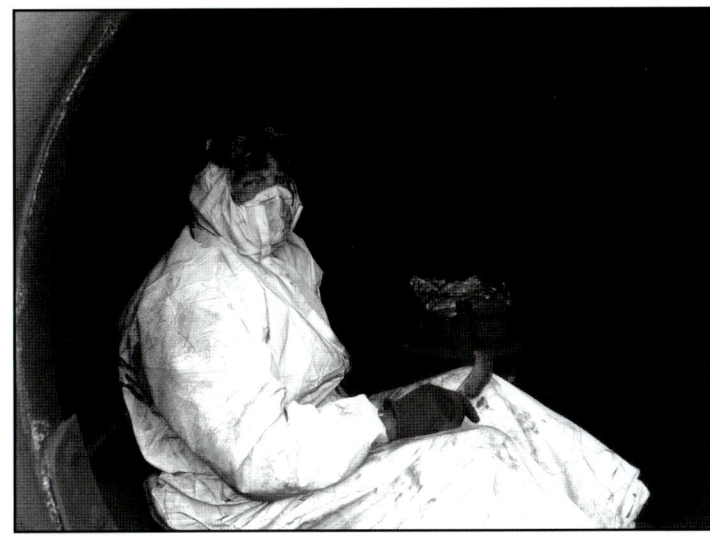

A tribute to FRT member the late Fred Jones who was always first to volunteer to undertake smokebox cleaning duties.
Photo: Tim Owen

11. FURNESS RAILWAY No. 20 TIMELINE

Furness Railway & Barrow Haematite Steel Co.

Date

23.12.1862	Furness Railway places order for FR 20
21.08.1863	FR 20 delivered to Furness Railway
25.05.1870	FR 20 purchased by BHSCo.
1915	FR 20 re-built with new boiler
09.07.1960	FR 20 displaced by diesels and retired
29.09.1960	Moved to George Hastwell School, Barrow
11.1983	Moved to Steamtown, Carnforth
1990	Purchased by the Lakeside Railway Society
1991	Transferred to the Furness Railway Trust
18.12.1996	Frames moved to VSEL, Barrow

Preservation Era Timeline

Date		Steamings
17.12.1998	Transferred from Barrow Shipyard to Haverthwaite	
13.01.1999	Passed steam test and return trip to Lakeside	35
20.04.1999	Formal launch after restoration	
03.08.1999	First Victorian Evening Special operated	
03.05.2000	To Keighley & Worth Valley Railway	5
25.05.2000	To Haverthwaite	8
12.09.2000	To North Yorkshire Moors Railway	
	Used for filming *Possession* movie	2
	Operated Pickering to Levisham for October Steam Gala	3
12.10.2000	To Haverthwaite	2
25.04.2001	To Barrow Hill Roundhouse Railway Centre	2
01.05.2001	To Midland Railway Centre	6
10.05.2001	To Haverthwaite	28
10.05.2004	To National Railway Museum, York for 2004 Railfest	9
	Operated passenger service on two days	
00.06.2004	To Haverthwaite	37
	Winter 2007/8 10 year Boiler Overhaul	
09.09.2008	To Tanfield Railway	2
	To *Locomotion*, Shildon	2
	To Beamish Museum	3
30.09.2008	To Haverthwaite	
22.02.2009	To *Locomotion*, Shildon	25
20.10.2009	To NRM York for nine steamings	9
04.11.2009	To *Locomotion*, Shildon	21
	Total carried forward	**199**

11. FURNESS RAILWAY No. 20 TIMELINE

Preservation Era Timeline (Continued)

Date	Event	Steamings
	Bought forward	199
25.05.2010	To Great Central Railway for 'Golden Oldies' Gala	6
08.06.2010	To Beamish Museum	19
02.08.2010	To Bluebell Railway for 50th Anniversary Gala	7
16.08.2010	To *Locomotion*, Shildon	28
24.05.2011	To Great Central Railway for 'Golden Oldies' Gala	4
01.06.2011	To *Locomotion*, Shildon	9
08.02.2012	To Ribble Steam Railway	11
01.05.2012	To Midland Railway Centre	3
11.05.2012	To Severn Valley Railway for *Kidderminster 150*	2
	Including hauling special train for the Duke of Gloucester	1
23.05.2012	To NRM, York for 2012 Railfest	9
14.06.2012	To Bluebell Railway	
	Used for filming *The Invisible Woman* movie	4
21.06.2012	To Middleton Railway for 200th Anniversary Celebrations	3
27.06.2012	To *Locomotion*, Shildon	63
21.08.2013	150th Birthday Celebrations	
22.10.2013	To Tyseley for Open Weekend	2
28.10.2013	To *Locomotion*, Shildon	129
21.10.2015	To Bo'ness & Kinneil Railway	2
29.10.2015	To *Locomotion*, Shildon	
07.05.2018	Final steaming at *Locomotion*, Shildon	
09.05.2018	To Ribble Steam Railway	2
08.07.2018	Final steaming before overhaul	
17.07.2021	Appeared at Barrow Festival of Transport	
11.10.2021	Passed steam test after overhaul	3
27.04.2022	To Buckinghamshire Railway Centre	2
05.05.2022	To Ribble Steam Railway	7
29.03.2023	To Didcot Railway Centre	9
06.04.2023	To Blaenavon's Heritage Railway	6
11.09.2023	To Ribble Steam Railway	7
10.07.2024	To West Somerset Railway for *Minehead 150*	5
07.08.2024	To Ribble Steam Railway	4
03.10.2024	To East Lancashire Railway	4
29.10.2024	To Ribble Steam Railway	6
01.05.2025	To Tanfield Railway	5
22.05.2025	To Ribble Steam Railway	
	Total to date	**561**

12. What Next?

With nearly another six years left on the current boiler ticket at the time of writing, the Furness Railway Trust is aiming to display Furness Railway No. 20 to as wide an audience as possible whilst recognising the limitations of operating a locomotive that is now over 160 years old. Some of the support crew are also not as young as they were when the FR 20 project started over 30 years ago and it is to be hoped that more young people will wish to become associated with the operation and maintenance of this historic engine to allow it to continue to steam for many years to come. There is also another challenge ahead with the FRT being bequeathed the components of BHSCo. No. 17, previously Furness Railway No. 25, by the estate of the late Bert Hitchen. These are in store at the Trust's base at the Ribble Steam Railway at Preston. The FRT in time wishes to honour Bert's intention to restore this engine to its Steelworks guise as a 0-4-0 saddle tank.

Anyone interested in supporting the Trust through being a member or perhaps joining the working parties in the modern workshop (heated by air source heat pump) at Preston is invited to contact the Membership Secretary: membership@furnessrailwaytrust.org.uk

A regular blog detailing current activities is accessible through the web site: furnessrailway.co.uk